SUMMARY: Measure What Matters

BY JOHN DOERR

QUALITY SUMMARIES

Table of Contents

Part One: OKRs in Action

Chapter One: Google, Meet OKRs

Before Google became the technology behemoth its known as today, John Doerr went to visit the fledgling company's headquarters in 1999. He had a good reason to visit. He had joined Google's board and had invested $11.8 million into the startup. He had been seduced by the confidence and determination of founders Larry Page and Sergey Brin and saw the same potential in Google as they did. Although Page and Brin had big visions and ideas, they lacked managerial experience and needed something to help them monitor and measure their progress. Doerr had the solution that would help them execute their idea. It was during that visit he introduced Google to OKRs.

Doerr explains that OKRs are objectives and key results. The two parts help individuals, teams, and whole organizations set goals and encourage people to work together to achieve the same aim. It looks at the 'what to do' and the 'how to do it'.

'Objective' describes what needs to be achieved and it should be an action-oriented goal that is concise, important, and inspirational. 'Key results' describe how the objective will be completed. It's a list of steps that outline what has to be done to accomplish the goal. Key results should be well-made, time-specific, measurable, and challenging. Doerr stresses that they should be quantitative and applied to a designated time period. If the OKR is well-defined from the beginning, then once all the key results are completed, then the objective is achieved.

Doerr discusses a paper published by the Harvard Business School that says strict goal setting could bring adverse effects, such as a narrow focus, decreased cooperation, and increased risk-taking. However, he argues that goals are undeniably necessary for optimal performance in a corporation. He underscores this point by adding that Edwin Locke, a psychology professor, said that difficult goals drive performance more effectively than easy goals and result in higher levels of output. Doerr also highlights the link between retention and engagement in work - the higher the engagement, the higher the retention. One of the most effective ways of increasing engagement is having clearly defined goals that help build job satisfaction and a stronger sense of unity. OKRs, says Doerr, also connect goals to the team's higher vision. They are motivating for employees as they celebrate milestones and also stretch an employee's skill set, allowing them to grow and be challenged.

It's not only large technology companies where OKRs are applicable. They are a survival tool for small startups because they help pull people together and makes concise plans to bring in much-needed funding in the initial stages of the company. In mid-sized organizations, OKRs help keep employees aligned and define expectations. In large corporations, they are the essential signals that coordinate direction and build unity between the diverse organizational members.

The effectiveness of OKRs is evident in the success of Google, yet Doerr lists further examples where OKRs are used in other companies, such as Dropbox, LinkedIn, and Oracle. He explains that Google continues to use OKRs and they are now a part of the daily fabric of the company. While other key factors such as solid leadership and value-centered culture were crucial in making Google one of the world's most valuable companies, OKRs certainly played an essential role too.

Chapter Two: Father of OKRs

In this chapter, Doerr introduces the 'father of OKRs', Andy Grove, with a story of how he first met him.

The story begins in Silicon Valley where Doerr managed to find a summer internship job at Intel. At that time, Grove worked at Intel as the executive vice president. During an Intel seminar that Doerr attended, Grove told a story about Fairchild, a company he once worked for. This company valued expertise and employed highly-skilled and knowledgeable staff, yet they failed to effectively convert that knowledge into solid results. Grove insisted that at Intel, the opposite would happen - implementing ideas was more important than knowledge. It was this mindset that underscored OKRs, Grove's most successful management tool.

The idea of goal-setting has been around for years, although in different forms from OKRs. Doerr takes a look at some of the past goal-setting organizations, including two of the most famous from the beginning of the 20th century - Frederick Winslow Taylor and Henry Ford. They were the first managers to systematically measure output and then use their findings to determine how to increase productivity. Their organizational structures were authoritarian and hierarchical, where the highest levels gave orders to subordinates who then dutifully carried them out.

Fifty years later, this evolved to Peter Drucker's take on goals which remained results-driven but more considerate to the employees. He developed a new management concept that respected and trusted workers, rather than seeing them as a means to make a profit. Drucker believed that employees should be involved in setting short and long-term goals through regular company-wide discussions. Drucker knew that when people are involved in setting goals, they are more likely to make sure it is accomplished. He published his theories and findings in his 1954 book, '*The Practice of Management*'. It was this book that provided the foundation of Grove's OKRs.

By the 1960s, the new concept of MBOs (management by objectives), that Drucker had advocated, had been embraced by several innovative enterprises, including Hewlett-Packard. However, many of the corporations that used MBOs created goals from the top and communicated them down the hierarchy or connected MBOs to financial initiatives. This weakened their value and rendered them less ineffective.

OKRs can be seen as improved MBOs. While they both focus on goal-setting, there are some striking differences. MBOs focus on the 'what to do', are set annually, are created in isolation by management at the top before being cascaded down to subordinates, are risk-averse, and are tied to financial initiatives. OKRs, on the other hand, focus on the 'what to do' and the 'how to do it', are set quarterly or monthly, are transparent, are created from the bottom-up or sideways, they aren't overly focused on compensation, and are aspirational. Doerr concludes with the key points of what makes an OKR effective, according to Grove. Three to five objectives per team or person are sufficient, and they should each be accompanied by a maximum of five key results. These OKRs should include input from the bottom to promote engagement and they ought to be cooperative, not dictatorial. OKRs are not set in stone and should be flexible to accommodate modifications or elimination of key results when necessary. They ought to be bold, aspirational, and challenge employees. At the same time, they should be treated as a tool, not as a measurement to use in performance reviews. Finally, OKRs take some time to fully adopt, so individuals, teams, and corporations need to remain patient and determined to make the most out of them.

Chapter Three: Operation Crush

Operation Crush was the name of Intel's survival strategy when it faced market threats from Motorola. They created an ambitious strategy that would place Intel back into the number one market position in microprocessors and squash Motorola's threatening presence.

Doerr highlights how OKRs were key in making this operation work, specifically in four key areas: focus, alignment, tracking, and stretching. Using OKRs helped the company focus on what they needed to do to reclaim their market position. They also helped Intel act with precision and speed.

In this chapter, Doerr lets Bill Davidson, Intel's head of microcomputer systems, tell the story of how Operation Crush was a success and the role OKRs played in this. Davidson, who led the operation, also coined the term 'as measured by' for Intel's OKRs. This provided a neat link between objective and key results. For example, 'the objective was achieved, as measured by the completion of the following key results'. Davidson explains that one of OKRs' main benefits during

Operation Crush was it shaped the company's behavior and got everyone pulling in the same direction. When he was first assigned the role of leading Operation Crush, Davidson says he felt the urgency to bring Intel back to a market leader, a feeling that was shared across the company. It was the 8086 microprocessor that was threatened by Motorola's presence and so Davidson and his team devised a strategy that would deflect the competitive challenge from the market.

First, Davidson recognized that there was no time to rebuild the 8086 or create any additional features. The strategy had to focus on the existing benefits of the microprocessor and highlight these to potential customers. First, they revamped marketing efforts by showing to customers the superiority of Intel's product family and its system-level performance. Then, they stressed its low cost of ownership and exceptional technical support from Intel's experts. All of these ideas were sent to the sales team to relay to their customers.

This planning and execution were completed in about two weeks. By the time Motorola had recognized Intel's comeback, it was too late and they were too slow to react. As a result, Intel regained its position as market leader in the microprocessor area.

Davidson credits the success of the operation to the way ideas were transformed into actions. Each objective at managerial level was measured by specific key results. These key results then became the objective of different departments, such as marketing and engineering. Each department could then set their own key results and relay these to individuals, who could, in turn, set their own steps to achieve objectives. The main advantage of OKRs is their ability to turn ideas into something tangible. In the case of Operation Crush, they were able to unify diverse areas, such as top management, different departments, and three geographic locations all into a total organizational effort. As Grove said, bad companies fail in times of crisis, yet great companies thrive.

Chapter Four: Superpower #1: Focus and Commit to Priorities

According to Doerr, OKRs have superpowers, which are qualities that make them superior. One of these superpowers is OKRs ability to get users focused and committed to certain priorities. It does this by having a narrow range of objectives (between three to five) which focus on the company's most important initiatives. Management need to decide which initiatives to pay attention to. As Grove said, by focusing on everything, we end up focusing on nothing. Having too many goals means we can't properly dedicate ourselves to what truly matters.

The best kind of goals is time-bound, as short-term goals help drive performance and motivation. If a company has annual goals, it's a good idea to break them down into quarterly objectives to enhance employee's focus and commitment. This is especially important in any organization that operates in the global marketplace. Quarterly goals allow companies to match the dynamic surrounding market with fast-paced goal-setting.

However, organizations shouldn't get too caught up in exact time periods. For example, it may make more sense to create OKRs in line with the product development cycle, if that's a priority for the company. In other words, OKRs work best when they fit within the culture and context of the corporation.

Doerr emphasizes this with two disastrous case studies of when OKRs were treated as one-dimensional tools. The first is the launch of the Ford Pinto in 1971, designed to compete against other budget and fuel-efficient cars in the market. The focus was strict and centered around a strategy of producing a low-cost, lightweight car. The company had three objectives that focused on size, cost, and appearance, yet ignored one vital factor - safety. In a bid to meet strict goals, the gas tank was fitted just inches away from the rear bumper, making the Ford Pinto a moving fire hazard. Adding any additional materials to prevent the danger was scrapped in order to make it lightweight. In the end, hundreds of people died in fire accidents in the Ford Pinto and the company had to recall its cars, costing the company millions of dollars.

Another example was with Wells Forge. Its strict, unattainable sales targets led bank managers to create fraudulent accounts in order to hit their goals. In the end, the company fired thousands of bank managers and suffered potentially irreversible damage to its brand image.

The stories highlight that the more ambitious an OKR, the higher the risk of missing important information. Less is more when it comes to OKRs.

Chapter Five: Focus: The Remind Story

In this chapter, Doerr uses the story of a company called Remind to highlight one of OKRs superior benefits - focus. Remind is a company that created a platform so students, parents, and teachers could better communicate between themselves and improve education. To find the right priorities to make the company grow, OKRs became essential.

Brett Kopf, a co-founder of Remind, unfolds his company's history and how OKR have played an important role in it. Kopf was diagnosed with ADHD and dyslexia from a young age and discovered that having one or two important goals helped him focus. His experience at school inspired him to set up Remind in order to shift the focus from accountability and curriculums to human connections.

In the beginning, it was a huge struggle trying to create a school system that could be accessed via mobile phones. However, participating in the Imagine K12, a start-up accelerator program for the educational market, was the turning point for developing a focus on what needed to be done. With the software in place, teachers could then sign in and start creating their own virtual classrooms. The project was a huge success: after three weeks, the company handled 130 thousand messages and they kept scaling until they reached six million users.

Kopf's goals until that point had been qualitative. He recognized the need to shift to more quantitative goals in order to better manage their rapidly scaling company. The company continued to grow from fourteen members of staff to 60, so having face-to-face meetings to discuss quarterly initiatives were no longer feasible.

The solution came from OKRs which helped everyone focus on the most important things and concentrate on moving the company forward. OKRs ensured everyone worked on one big idea at a time. Management would vote for the top quarterly objectives and then relay them to other staff, explaining why these were important and deciding together how to accomplish them. The OKRs provided several significant benefits for Remind, says Kopf. They took the politics out of goal-setting, made all goals transparent and known throughout the organization, and helped prevent micromanagement.

He adds that in the beginning, they were over-ambitious and

started with seven or eight OKRs when they only had the capacity for two at the most. OKRs are simple to use, he says, but implementing them can take time.

Chapter Six: The Nuna Story

This chapter presents the Nuna story, another business that shows how OKRs can be used to enforce commitment. As well as focus, commitment is another important element in the first of the four OKR superpowers.

Jini Kim made Nuna from the desire to deliver Americans with better health care. Prior to starting Nuna, she had worked at Google where she had learned about OKRs. She completely believed in their effectiveness for goal-setting and bringing an organization together, and so wanted to apply them to Nuna.

She first tried implementing OKRs in Nuna in 2015, yet she realized that many workers simply didn't make individual goals and few people committed to their objectives. She learned that getting people to accept OKRs was a gradual process and that the executives needed to commit to them if there was any hope of getting other employees on board.

She tried again in 2016 and this time, she kept on top of everyone, insisting they set their individual goals and encouraging leaders to inspire others by practicing what they were teaching. Kim set herself goals and kept them open and transparent, in order to show that she too was accountable for her work. Slowly but surely, the incremental change to OKRs worked and the company adopted the process.

As Nuna expanded, the company came to rely on OKRs more than ever. Kim reflects how OKRs encourage important conversations, pull people together, and enforce commitment among everyone. It won't work the first time, she says. But stick with it and the results will be worth it.

Chapter Seven: Superpower #2: Align And Connect For Teamwork

The importance of teamwork is emphasized in this chapter, especially cross-functional coordination. It's considered superior to individual work for advanced problem solving and innovation and it helps the company work quicker and more efficiently. Cross-functional coordination is dependent on horizontal links. The best way to achieve this, according to Doerr, is by using a transparent OKR system that sets goals both from the top-down and from the bottom-up.

Transparent goals are essential to keep the company moving forward as public goals are more likely to be achieved than private ones. It also helps collaboration: when goals are open to all, colleagues can see when fellow workers are struggling and offer their support. This, in turn, improves overall productivity and deepens work relations between staff.

Top-down goal-setting is when the objectives and key results come from the top management and are trickled down through the hierarchy. The key results of management's objectives become the objectives of the next level in the hierarchy. This pattern continues throughout all the layers. There are some disadvantages of having top-down only goals. If all the objectives are cascaded down, it can make goal-setting mechanical and cumbersome. If a goal needs to be changed, it means all the goals further down the hierarchy will also need to be readjusted and updated. The slow nature of top-down goals can minimize frequent goal-setting. It also silences those at the front-end of the business - for example, the sales team - who could offer valuable insights. It also makes horizontal communication complicated. Goals improve overall performance, but not when they have to move up and down the hierarchy.

The best type of OKRs, says Doerr, are those that are transparent and an equal mix of top-down and bottom-up. This allows objectives and key results to skip layers in the hierarchy while encouraging insights outside of the C-suite. It fosters an environment where everyone takes responsibility for their own objectives. It also minimizes micromanagement and encourages more autonomy.

Chapter Eight: Align: The MyFitnessPal Story

This chapter looks at some of the most important lessons that MyFitnessPal discovered from its early days as a startup to its challenging merger with Under Armour. One of the key factors in the company's success was the use of OKRs. They helped create goals to keep everyone focused on the overall mission and unify the different cultures between MyFitnessPal and Under Armour.

MyFitnessPal was co-founded by Mike and Arthur Lee who developed the app as a way for people to track what they eat and measure how effectively they exercise. The app allows them to set personal fitness goals and contact with like-minded people through the platform.

In this chapter, Mike Lee tells the story of MyFitnessPal's growth. One of the first lessons he learned with goal-setting is how company size makes a big difference when it comes to goal-setting. In the early days as a small startup, goals were highly measurable and the team focused on one goal at a time.

However, once the company began to scale quickly, they needed to start focusing on multiple goals in order to move forward at the required pace. It was then they introduced OKRs to the organization.

After implementing OKRs in MyFitnessPal, Lee learned several valuable lessons. First, implementing the OKR process is hard and it takes time and effort to create the right goals and spread them throughout the company. He also explains that although their OKRs were well-made, their implementation was less successful due to a lack of alignment between departments. They managed to fix this by having meetings that openly explained their OKRs and made the objectives transparent. He stresses that when making alignment, this doesn't necessarily mean that two departments or teams share the same key results. They may have parallel objectives but they will each have distinct key results, as this is the way to ensure accountability between the two. He also noticed that the more ambitious the objective, the more likely staff would make conservative key results. In this case, it's important to clarify expectations (such as, 'it's ok to take a risk with this goal.') or make adjustments to the objective.

When MyFitnessPal merged with Under Armour, Lee learned the larger the organization, the more value OKRs offer. This is because they help the alignment of diverse teams and expectations. It took 18 months for MyFitnessPal and Connected Fitness, Under Armour's new division, to align their goals. However, they managed in the end, thanks to OKRs, says Lee. Nowadays, MyFitnessPal is well-established yet they still use OKRs to manage their goals and prioritize what matters. By using specific metrics, they decide what goals would make the most impact in the following quarter and that helps them narrow down their focus for the next few months. They understand they can't do everything and in order to succeed, they need to focus on just a handful of important objectives at a time.

Chapter Nine: The Intuit Story

Some of the key features of OKRs are that they are open and visible to the entire organization at every level of every department. If implemented correctly, they will make the OKR-using company more coherent.

This is one of the qualities that has made Intuit, a financial software company that regularly features in Forbes, survive external technological threats and go on to thrive. It operates under a culture of transparency, adaptability, and connectedness. All of these qualities are a perfect fit for OKRs and complement the company's core values.

OKRs are challenging to implement in the beginning and one way of introducing them is to run a pilot project. This allows any kinks to be ironed out before applying them to the entire company. This was something Intuit did by introducing OKRs to help the IT department tackle the move to cloud systems.

At the time, the company was moving in several directions at once and needed some structure. The company felt it was important that this new style of goal-setting was accepted enthusiastically, rather than forcing employees to comply with it.

To do this, managers met once a month to discuss individual goals, compare notes, and provide feedback. This would help ensure the OKRs were still relevant and progressing in the right direction. In the IT department, each person had three to five business objectives of their own as well as one or two personal ones. Leaders would also have personal goals and would share them with subordinates.

Intuit operates globally and by extending OKRs to different global locations, everyone knew what others were doing and it allowed for facilitated global collaboration using online collaboration tools.

All of these steps to implement OKRS fit well with Intuit's culture and helps motivate frontline employees as they can see how their work aligns with the company's overall goals. As a horizontal company that fosters a collaborative culture, it is a breeding ground for innovation, superior communication, and easy coordination. These qualities are enhanced by using OKRs.

Chapter Ten: Superpower #3: Track for Accountability

The beauty about OKRs, according to Doerr, is that they can be tracked and adapted as circumstances change. In comparison, traditional goals are set and then tend to be forgotten. OKRs' flexibility is one of its major strengths. Doerr identifies three phases of the OKR life cycle.

The first is 'The Setup'. This is the initial stage of OKR implementation and it emphasizes the importance of having the right tools for the job. Everyday software doesn't allow OKRs to scale. For example, if a huge company recorded all their goals in a word file, there would be thousands of individual documents, making it infeasible to search through them all for connections or alignment. The best way to record goals is to adopt a cloud-based OKR management software system that makes it easier to track, edit, and measure OKRs. These types of platforms make everyone's goals visible, drive engagement, promote internal networking, saves time and money, and minimizes frustration.

In order for the OKR system to work, it must be adopted universally by the entire company. One way of doing this is to select a couple of employees for the role of 'OKR Shepherd'. They are responsible for getting everyone involved and monitoring people's commitment.

The second stage is 'Midlife Tracking'. Making measured progress can be a great motivator. In fact, it can be more motivating than monetary incentives, public recognition, and even achieving the goal itself. OKRs are adaptable and at any point in the cycle employees can continue, update, launch a new goal, or discontinue the OKR. If it's decided that this OKR is no longer relevant and will be stopped, this must be communicated to everyone dependent on it.

The final stage is 'Wrap-up: Rinse and Repeat'. This is the post-evaluation stage once the OKR has been completed. It includes three important parts. The first is 'scoring' which allows the performance of each key result to be scored and quantified. The second is 'self-assessment' which lets the employee conduct a subjective judgment on their own work, learn from setbacks, and celebrate successes. Finally, 'reflection' encourages time to consider the lessons learned from the OKRs. For example, the individual can reflect on what contributed to their success, what obstacles they faced, how they would rewrite the goal if they had the opportunity, and what they have learned that will influence their approach to the next OKR cycle.

Chapter Eleven: Track: The Gates Foundation Story

OKRs have an inbuilt tracking system that allows users to monitor progress and check performance. The importance of this feature is highlighted in this chapter using the story of the Bill & Melinda Gates Foundation.

As a $20 billion startup, this foundation was the first of its kind. It had an ambitious mission - to bring a healthy and productive life for everyone. As Gates still played an important role at Microsoft, there was a lot at stake and a lot to do. Tracking became essential.

Gates had always aimed high when setting goals. At Microsoft, he set the target of creating a computer for every desk and in every home. Competitors didn't think that way as they didn't believe it was possible. Yet Microsoft believed scaling would make things cheaper and therefore possible. Gates treated goal-setting at the foundation the same way as he did in Microsoft.

Within two years of starting, the foundation had scaled

enormously and needed more structured goal setting. This is where OKRs stepped in and provided the structure they needed to accomplish their ambitious plans. Goals were big but realistic. If any were too aspirational, they were adjusted as inflated ideas can affect credibility. OKRs allowed the foundation to be both ambitious and disciplined.

Gates says that in goal making, it's common to see people confusing objectives with 'mission'. The mission is directional and inspiring. Objectives are concrete steps to engage in and, while they are inspiring too, they are realistic and grounded.

Chapter Twelve: Superpower #4: Stretch for Amazing

This chapter looks at 'stretch goals', the ones that push us beyond our comfort zones and help make creative solutions and transform business models. They are the key to innovation and moving forward.

OKRs can be stretch goals. For example, Google has two types of goals. The first are committed goals which are tied with specific metrics. They are achieved 100% of the time and within a specific time frame. The second are aspirational goals, which are made for high risk, big ideas. They are challenging and have a much higher failure rate - Google expects a 40% failure rate with aspirational goals.

Aspirational goals - or stretch goals - are linked to a higher level of performance. The harder the goal, the superior the performance, even though they are not achieved all of the time. These stretch goals stretch the ability of workers and can make them more productive, motivated, and engaged. It enhances interest in the task at hand and can foster an entrepreneurial environment.

These stretch goals draw from all of the OKRs superpowers. They require focus and commitment to find ways to achieve the challenging target. In order to be achieved, they must be tackled in an environment of transparency and connectedness. They also depend on tracking to know if the stretched objective has been achieved.

It's important that stretch goals are still realistic. If they are set too high so they end up ignoring reality, they will create adverse effects such as demotivation and frustration. In order to be achieved, leaders also need to convey how important the outcome of the goals is and fuel the belief that it is attainable. Companies such as Google love aspirational goals as it keeps them ahead of the game. However, not all companies use them. For example, MtFitnessPal considers all their OKRs to be committed goals and 100% achievable. While that works for them, having some goals with even a moderate stretch is a good idea to keep the company ahead and allow innovation. There is no 'magic number' for the right stretch, but Doerr suggests to consider what 'amazing' looks like and aim for that.

Chapter Thirteen: Stretch: The Google Chrome Story

Google is full of stories of both successful and failed aspirational goals. This chapter looks at the development of Google Chrome and how stretched OKRs made it become the browser it is today. If the goals had all been committed and allowed no room for failure, then it wouldn't have developed the way it had.

Sundar Pichai was the Vice President of product development at Google and he was in charge of taking Google Chrome to the next level and to the market. There were already other browsers on the market so Chrome had to be significantly different to the others to make it worthwhile. He used stretched OKRs to make it amazing and set ambitious goals. Although failure is sometimes expected with stretched OKRs, that doesn't mean it's ok not to meet them. Google recognizes that innovation goes hand-in-hand with failure, yet it still expects to see the drive to succeed in their employees. Pichai had to set high goals and prove he was working towards them. His first goal was to get 20 million weekly active users by the end of the year - an ambitious goal since the browser was starting from zero. However, it set the expectations and got everyone motivated.

Leaders must challenge their team without making them feel the goal is unachievable. Pichai used this goal to push the limit of his team (and himself), give direction, keep everyone questioning ideas, and to eliminate any chance of complacency.

Stretch OKRs involve extreme problem-solving. When coupled with big numbers, they can seem abstract and unreal in the beginning. However, this is where trackability comes in handy. By breaking them down into measurable objectives for each year and then per quarter, the goal becomes a lot more doable. OKRs give the benefit of creating clear, quantitative targets while taking giant qualitative leaps.

Pichai's goals became steadily more and more ambitious - yet they were succeeding. One of their new goals was to get to 111 million active users. They encountered problems at times, yet whenever that happened, they would think about how they could do things differently. After a successful marketing campaign to increase product awareness, they finally reached their goal.

Nowadays, Chrome has more than 1 billion active users on

mobile alone. It was thanks to OKRs keeping them focused and stretching the team's capabilities were they able to achieve such staggering success.

Chapter Fourteen: Stretch: The YouTube Story

OKRs are a major part of Google's culture. The second 'stretch goal' success story from Google relates to YouTube.

The woman behind YouTube's success was Susan Wojcicki. She was the one that convinced the board at Google to acquire YouTube after she saw the potential in online video and felt it would disrupt network TV. Once Google had bought YouTube, it needed some stretch goals to make it work. The first was a four-year goal to reach 1 billion hours of YouTube viewing time per day. The second was to do it responsibly.

The first challenge was to define a metric that allowed them to measure YouTube's success. The number of views was the first obvious metric, yet they soon realized there was a better one - the length of watch time. The number of viewership doesn't measure the quality of the content, whereas the watch time does. This makes it better for advertising and encourages more responsible growth.

The 1-billion-hour mark was a stretched goal that pushed

everyone to their limits. It seemed like an enormous, unattainable figure. However, reframing that goal helped make it seem more achievable. One of the managers, Shishir Mehrotra, broke it down and explained 1 billion viewing hours is actually 20% of the world's total TV time. It placed the number into perspective and helped people realize there are still bigger things out there than their goal.

Although the watch hours were growing and the OKRs were well-crafted, they still weren't quite on target. However, they continued to grow responsibly by providing quality user-made content and professional videos and removing click-bait from the main pages. The team wasn't sure if they would hit the 1 billion mark, yet in October, a couple of months before the end of the target year, they met their objective.

When it comes to stretched goals, it's important to have support from the top and for employees to feel that the top management believes in their project and ability. To reach ambitious goals, it's vital that everyone is aligned and focused around the same objective. This is where OKRs are especially useful as it pulls everyone together and gets everybody working towards the same objective.

Wojcicki believes they couldn't have achieved what they had achieved with YouTube without the clarity, structure, and process that stretch OKRs provide. It gives a benchmark to measure performance against, which is something people need to stay on track. They are also flexible enough to accommodate changes. For example, when YouTube was growing, the main metric was watch-time hours. Nowadays, they are looking at other variables that could measure the YouTube experience, such as web-added videos and viewer satisfaction. As OKRs are highly adaptable, these metrics can easily be tested using a solid, goal-setting framework. Wojcicki adds that OKRs are especially useful for young companies beginning to build their culture as they help make it clear where they are going. However, no company is too young or too old to adopt OKRs; no company is too late. Although it's better to have the rules established from the beginning, even mature companies can adopt new processes. Stretch goals are motivating and create a sense of urgency by committing to transformative improvement. YouTube is evidence of this. Once a struggling video platform, it now has more than one billion users which represent around one-third of all users on the internet. It can be accessed from more than eighty countries and can be watched in more than seventy languages. This wasn't luck that this happened - it was down to well-crafted OKRs that demanded structure, discipline, attention to details, and precise execution.

Part Two: The New World of Work

Chapter Fifteen: Continuous Performance Management: Okrs and Cfrs

This chapter looks at ways of improving the traditional annual performance reviews. These performance reviews are often considered costly, fruitless, and tiring. Doerr stresses that workplace communication needs to be improved and that a new HR model is required.

The new system is the modern-day alternative to annual reviews and it is known as Continuous Performance Management. It's implemented using CFRs, which are Conversations, Feedback, and Recognition.

CFRs include many of the same qualities as OKRs, such as transparency, empowerment, teamwork, and accountability across all layers of the organization. CFRs can gain a rich overview of the success of specific OKRs and provide unique insights into overall performance. In this sense, CFRs and OKRs are mutually reinforcing.

The Continuous Performance Management process can improve transparency and increase alignment. It replaces annual reviews with ongoing conversations and real-time feedback. It also works to elevate performance, increase morale, and boost personal development. Rather than focusing on outcomes like annual reviews, it focuses on progress.

Conversation in CFRs looks at changing the dialogue of annual reviews. It cuts the connection of goal achievement and compensation because when goals are rewarded monetarily, it can reduce the challenge of the goals and prevent people from stretching themselves. Managers and employees meet regularly for one-to-one meetings to reflect on performance, goal setting, progress updates, career growth, and two-way coaching.

Feedback is a vital part of CFRs as is directly tied with OKRs. It keeps people on track and motivated, and it helps draw out the most of using OKRs. Feedback between managers and employees should include discussing goals and tracking progress, and it should make the employees feel empowered and inspired. The way to do this is to offer highly constructive feedback and mix it with peer-feedback, especially in cross-functional teams.

The final part of CFRs is recognition. Recognition should be performance-based and horizontal as these qualities make it especially engaging. There are several ways to implement recognition and each company may have their own unique way of doing it. However, common ways include peer-to-peer recognition, share recognition stories among staff, recognize people for actions and overall outcomes rather than just numbers, tie recognition to the company's goals and strategies so people can see how they themselves contributed, and celebrate all the small things so recognition becomes frequent and attainable.

Chapter Sixteen: Ditching Annual Performance Reviews: The Adobe Story

This chapter compares Adobe's past and present ways of evaluating performance. In the past, Adobe spent eight hours with each employee in annual performance reviews. They decided to get rid of this way and adopt more frequent, forward-thinking reviews.

They started doing multiple check-in conversations per year between managers and subordinates, which included a flexible and transparent meeting with no tracking, no paperwork, and minimal structure. Each meeting was centered on three areas: OKRs, regular feedback, and career development and growth. Feedback was ongoing and wasn't limited to a once a year meeting. Instead, with continuous feedback, employees could keep on top of their progress and their performance could be monitored and evaluated quicker. Managers were given budgets to decide bonuses themselves, which empowered them. They rewarded employees based on wider criteria, including how performance impacted business, the scarcity of their skills, the market conditions, and other factors. With no more fixed compensation, teammates were no longer competitors, which created a more open, transparent environment.

To make a Continuous Performance Management system work, it depends on three important requirements. These are executive support, clarity of the company's objectives and how they align with the individual's priorities, and investment in training to give managers and leaders skills to effectively give constructive, corrective feedback and reward employees accordingly.

Chapter Seventeen: Baking Better Every Day: The Zume Pizza Story

This chapter emphasizes the importance of OKRs and CFRs, especially when used together. They are proven tools that contribute to high performance and growth. There also promote subtle yet important effects, such as better preparing executives for leadership positions and allowing less communicative employees a chance to excel. It also helps improve the organization as a whole in many different areas. OKRs and CFRs teach leaders to become better communicators and motivate employees. It makes all the staff become more disciplined. It promotes a structured goal setting that can help teach people to work within constraints. Zume, a fast-food company that sells artisanal pizzas made by robots, is an example of how OKRs and the values of Continuous Performance Management can help a company grow in the right direction. Zume was an ambitious project, which required it to have focused operations and aligned staff.

By selling pizzas made by robots, they were able to invest more capital in higher quality ingredients and innovation. Their company grew quickly and they suddenly found there were too many things to do and too many people to manage. Operations stopped being smooth and prioritizing became a challenge. Management found that Zume's biggest asset was its innovative and skilled team. Each individual worked wholeheartedly on what they thought was the most important idea - however, the team wasn't always working together and different tasks were being worked on at the same time.

The more people, the greater the chance of misalignment. However, by introducing OKRs soon after launching Zume, it helped align the operations and the direction of people. It also helped train executives and managers on how to manage a business within limits and resource restraints. It helped them keep a focus on what they could and couldn't do. By instilling a sense of discipline in the company, OKRs encouraged people to be more thoughtful about what they could achieve and take a step back to think about the most important things to be focusing.

The advantage of using OKRs from the beginning is that it trains leaders to think in an OKR culture. Without OKRs, companies may scale too quickly and leaders can't cope with the increased demands. The company fails to meet its objectives and dies. The other possibility is that the company grows, leaders fail to meet the new challenges associated with growth, and are replaced by leaders who can. Neither situation is ideal but can be avoided by having a strong sense of goal-setting and a transparent organization from the start. For Zume, OKRs removed ambiguity and made room for clear goal-setting and engagement from everyone. When first using OKRs, the process is uncertain yet the more people get used to them, the more collaborative and efficient the organizational environment becomes. It creates better transparency, better teamwork, better conversation, and a better culture. It ensures people are talking about the same thing and helps establish a common framework for decision making. By having all goals out in the open, it makes everyone equal and gives voices to even the least vocal of the team members.

Chapter Eighteen: Culture

This chapter explores the importance of culture at work. Culture, says Doerr, is what gives work meaning. An important part of culture is OKRs and CFRs and these can be used as tools for cultural change. How? OKRs are ways for leaders to define their priorities and insights. CFRs ensure that these priorities and insights are transmitted throughout the company.

Defining a positive culture is tricky, admits Doerr, yet OKRs and CFRs provide a template. They align teams and assist them to work towards a common goal. They create transparency and accountability and push for higher performance. A healthy culture and structured goals are mutually dependent.

A strong culture is essential as it creates efficiency, speed, and reliable decisions. An OKR culture is an example of strong, accountable culture. It creates an environment of transparency and alignment that make people more conscientious about meeting their objectives. In an OKR culture, employees don't complete their OKRs because their boss pushes them; rather they do it because it's important to the company and other people depend on them.

There are two main factors in creating a high-motivation culture. These are catalysts (in other words, OKRs) and nourishers (in other words, CFRs). The OKRs give clarity and purpose to strategies and plans, whereas the CFRs supply the push to make it happen and encourage top management to treat employees as partners. Companies that value their employees, will often have the best sales and best customer service.

The most successful companies have a culture that encourages the organization to inspire their workers rather than simply engage them. It also turns rules into shared principles, builds trust to encourage risk-taking, pushes for innovation to drive performance and productivity, and swaps compensation for a sense of purpose.

The most powerful cultural force of all, concludes Doerr, is transparency. As an OKR and CFR culture values transparency, it underscores the importance of the connection between cultural change and structured goal setting.

Chapter Nineteen: Culture Change: The Lumeris Story

This chapter tells the story of Lumeris, a company that provides software, service, and knowledge to the healthcare network. It highlights how sometimes, the organizational culture isn't ready to adopt OKRs and any attempt to implement them won't work. The culture needs to be open and ready for total transparency and accountability in order for OKRs to work. If it isn't in that stage, then a cultural transformation is required. This was the case with Lumeris. Lumeris had all the structure for OKRs. Its implementation looked great on the surface. However, in reality, it wasn't working and people weren't committed to using OKRs. The underlying problem was that people didn't trust the OKR system and weren't convinced by its benefits. If the environment didn't change and the cultural barriers were left unchecked, then the OKR system wasn't going to succeed. The first step in implementing OKRs was to take a big step back and focus on getting a cultural alignment. This included getting rid of leaders who held an autocratic mindset that wasn't compatible with OKRs. The leaders were replaced by executives who could communicate the values of OKRs and convince people that Lumeris would now reward collaboration, transparency, and shared accountability. These were the new values of the company.

The issue with cultural transformation is that it can take months and even years to properly implement, adapt, and live the new cultural values of the organization. This was the case with Lumeris. It took them about 18 months to replace 85% of the HR professionals and a further three years to build up the middle management. However, after this time, the new culture was ready.

Once the new culture was established, the company were able to try reintroducing OKRs into the structure. It's not an easy process and not instantaneous. In Lumeris's case, they had already tried OKRs once and had failed, so they had the added challenge of convincing people that this time it would work. Additionally, it's essential to reprogram the way people think about failure. Rather than it being something to be ashamed of and hidden, management needed to show that having OKRs - and consequent potential failure - out in the open for all to see is not a bad thing. It took time, but nowadays, Lumeris has a culture based on connectivity and coordination.

Chapter Twenty: Culture Change: Bono's ONE Campaign Story

When Bono, U2's lead singer, co-founded DATA (Debt, AIDS, Trade, Africa), he was on a mission to address poverty and development in Africa and campaign for policy change. This chapter looks at the way Bono used OKRs to maximize performance both in DATA and its related ONE Campaign. As ONE grew, it relied heavily on OKRs to help achieve the fundamental culture change it needed to make it function. Before OKRs, Bono had a clear vision for DATA. He saw what seemed like an impossible objective, described the plan, and then figured out how to get there.

However, as it grew, it needed more measurable processes and quantitative results. One of the main issues DATA had was that it had too many goals and it wanted to achieve too much. The goals became so big, that people became confused as to what they should do and how they should do it. Bono says that OKRs forced them to think more clearly about their aims and agree as a team what they could do with the resources that they had. It gave them a framework to build their ideas around and helped hone their strategy, execution, and outcomes.

They were trying to help thousands of people in Africa. However, they realized that they needed to better understand what these people truly needed. At that time, the campaign was marching forward doing what they thought was best, rather than checking with African locals what was actually required. In order to address this issue, they needed to commit to organizational and cultural change to allow increased collaboration with African leaders. By listening to those who live in Africa and are affected by the problems there, ONE could better redirect their efforts to help people more effectively, such as tackling corruption.

Bono was fuelled by a passion to make DATA succeed, yet it was OKRs that help steer him in the right way to make it work. Doerr also highlights that if all OKRs are green - in other words, successful - then this is a sign that the OKRs need to be modified. It's ok to have red - or failed - OKRs as these show the company is moving towards bigger and more ambitious goals. It creates an environment of trust and risk in which failing is not considered the end of the world. It cultivates a safe place to be innovative and test ideas.

Chapter Twenty-One: The Goals to Come

The final chapter ends with some final words from Doerr. He emphasizes that ideas are easy; execution is everything. This idea is at the heart of OKRs.

The chapter reiterates that OKRs and CFRs can help organizations of all sizes, backgrounds, and status. They can be used to stimulate workers, to unify teams, to develop and grow leaders, and to track the most important priorities. Doerr finishes with his hopes for OKRs. He sees them as tools that can be used beyond helping organizations. He sees their potential in helping GDP growth, health care, schools, social progress, and government performance. Their adaptability can be leveraged to measure what truly matters the most.

Key Takeaways

- OKRs are objectives and key results. The two parts help individuals, teams, and whole organizations set goals and encourage people to work together to achieve the same aim. It looks at the 'what to do' and the 'how to do it'.

- 'Objective' describes what needs to be achieved and it should be an action-oriented goal that is concise, important, and inspirational.

- 'Key results' describe how the objective will be completed. It's a list of steps that outline what has to be done to accomplish the goal. Key results should be well-made, time-specific, measurable, and challenging. Doerr stresses that they should be quantitative and applied to a designated time period.

- If the OKR is well-defined from the beginning, then once all the key results are completed, then the objective is achieved.

- OKRs, says Doerr, also connect goals to the team's higher vision. They are motivating for employees as they celebrate milestones and also stretch an employee's skill set, allowing them to grow and be challenged.

- OKRs focus on the 'what to do' and the 'how to do it', are set quarterly or monthly, are transparent, are created from the bottom-up or sideways, they aren't overly focused on compensation, and are aspirational.

- Three to five objectives per team or person are sufficient, and they should each be accompanied by a maximum of five key results. These OKRs should include input from the bottom to promote engagement and they ought to be cooperative, not dictatorial.

- OKRs are not set in stone and should be flexible to accommodate modifications or elimination of key results when necessary. They ought to be bold, aspirational, and challenge employees.

- At the same time, they should be treated as a tool, not as a measurement to use in performance reviews.

- Finally, OKRs take some time to fully adopt, so individuals, teams, and corporations need to remain patient and determined to make the most out of them.

- The main advantage of OKRs is their ability to turn ideas into something tangible.

- Bad companies fail in times of crisis, yet great companies thrive.

- Quarterly goals allow companies to match the dynamic surrounding market with fast-paced goal-setting.

- However, organizations shouldn't get too caught up in exact time periods. For example, it may make more sense to create OKRs in line with the product development cycle, if that's a priority for the company. In other words, OKRs work best when they fit within the culture and context of the corporation.

- Superpower #1: Focus and Commit to Priorities
- OKRs have superpowers, which are qualities that make them superior. One of these superpowers is OKRs ability to get users focused and committed to certain priorities. It does this by having a narrow range of objectives (between three to five) which focus on the company's most important initiatives. Management need to decide which initiatives to pay attention to.

- Superpower #2: Align and Connect for Teamwork
- Cross-functional coordination is dependent on horizontal links. The best way to achieve this, according to Doerr, is by using a transparent OKR system that sets goals both from the top-down and from the bottom-up.

- Superpower #3: Track for Accountability
- OKRs can be tracked and adapted as circumstances change. OKRs' flexibility is one of its major strengths. Doerr identifies three phases of the OKR life cycle.
- The first is 'The Setup'. This is the initial stage of OKR implementation and it emphasizes the importance of having the right tools for the job.
- The second stage is 'Midlife Tracking'. Making measured progress can be a great motivator. OKRs are adaptable and at any point in the cycle employees can continue, update, launch a new goal, or discontinue the OKR. If it's decided that this OKR is no longer relevant and will be stopped, this must be communicated to everyone dependent on it.
- The final stage is 'Wrap-up: Rinse and Repeat'. This is the post-evaluation stage once the OKR has been completed. It includes three important parts. The first is 'scoring' which allows the performance of each key result to be scored and quantified. The second is 'self-assessment' which lets the employee conduct a subjective judgment on their own work, learn from setbacks, and celebrate successes. Finally, 'reflection' encourages time to consider the lessons learned

from the OKRs.

- Superpower #4: Stretch for Amazing
- OKRs can be stretch goals. For example, Google has two types of goals. The first are committed goals which are tied with specific metrics. They are achieved 100% of the time and within a specific time frame. The second are aspirational goals, which are made for high risk, big ideas. They are challenging and have a much higher failure rate - Google expects a 40% failure rate with aspirational goals.
- It's important that stretch goals are still realistic. If they are set too high so they end up ignoring reality, they will create adverse effects such as demotivation and frustration. In order to be achieved, leaders also need to convey how important the outcome of the goals is and fuel the belief that it is attainable.
- Stretch OKRs involve extreme problem-solving. When coupled with big numbers, they can seem abstract and unreal in the beginning. However, this is where trackability comes in handy. By breaking them down into measurable objectives for each year and then per quarter, the goal becomes a lot more doable. OKRs give the benefit of creating clear, quantitative targets while taking giant qualitative leaps.

- OKRs are challenging to implement in the beginning and one way of introducing them is to run a pilot project. This allows any kinks to be ironed out before applying them to the entire company.

- The new system is the modern-day alternative to annual reviews and it is known as Continuous Performance Management. It's implemented using CFRs, which are Conversations, Feedback, and Recognition.

- To make a Continuous Performance Management system

work, it depends on three important requirements. These are executive support, clarity of the company's objectives and how they align with the individual's priorities, and investment in training to give managers and leaders skills to effectively give constructive, corrective feedback and reward employees accordingly.

- Culture, says Doerr, is what gives work meaning. An important part of culture is OKRs and CFRs and these can be used as tools for cultural change. How? OKRs are ways for leaders to define their priorities and insights. CFRs ensure that these priorities and insights are transmitted throughout the company.

- There are two main factors in creating a high-motivation culture. These are catalysts (in other words, OKRs) and nourishers (in other words, CFRs). The OKRs give clarity and purpose to strategies and plans, whereas the CFRs supply the push to make it happen and encourage top management to treat employees as partners. Companies that value their employees, will often have the best sales and best customer service.

- Ideas are easy; execution is everything. This idea is at the

  heart of OKRs.

Final Words

This book is a treasure trove of quality business advice. To ensure the lessons stick, I like to go over just the key takeaways once a week. I do this for this book and all the other summaries I've wrote to ensure the key principles are really engrained into my mind and soon become natural habits and reactions in my every day life.

Thanks for checking out my book. I hope you found this of value and enjoyed it. But before you go, I have one small favor to ask…

Would you take 60 seconds and write a review about this book?

Reviews are the best way for independent authors (like me) to get noticed, sell more books, and it gives me the motivation to continue producing. I also read every review and use the feedback to write future revisions – and even future books.

Thanks again.

CPSIA information can be obtained
at www.ICGtesting.com
Printed in the USA
BVHW030033040219
539386BV00001B/48/P